What if we do N**O**THING?

EARTH'S
GARBAGE CRISIS

Christiane Dorion

**Consultant: Rob Bowden, Specialist in
Global Environmental and Social Issues**

WORLD ALMANAC® LIBRARY

Please visit our web site at: www.garethstevens.com
For a free color catalog describing World Almanac® Library's list of
high-quality books and multimedia programs, call 1-800-848-2928 (USA)
or 1-800-387-3178 (Canada). World Almanac® Library's fax: (414) 332-3567.

Library of Congress Cataloging-in-Publication Data

Dorion, Christiane.
    Earth's garbage crisis / Christiane Dorion.
      p. cm. – (What if we do nothing?)
    Includes bibliographical references and index.
    ISBN-13: 978-0-8368-7753-3 (lib. bdg.)
    ISBN-13: 978-0-8368-8153-0 (softcover)
    1. Refuse and refuse disposal–Juvenile literature.   2. Pollution–Juvenile literature.
  3. Refuse and refuse disposal–Environmental aspects–Juvenile literature.   I. Title.
  TD792.D67   2007
  363.72'8–dc22   2006030443

First published in 2007 by
World Almanac® Library
A Member of the WRC Media Family of Companies
330 West Olive Street, Suite 100
Milwaukee, WI 53212 USA

Produced by Arcturus Publishing Limited
Editor: Nicola Barber
Designer: Peta Phipps

World Almanac® Library editorial direction: Valerie J. Weber
World Almanac® Library editor: Leifa Butrick
World Almanac® Library art direction: Tammy West
World Almanac® Library graphic design: Charlie Dahl
World Almanac® Library production: Jessica Yanke and Robert Kraus

Picture credits: CORBIS: cover bottom inset (Koopman), 5 (Ashley Cooper), 6 (Bob Sacha),
10 (Reuters), 17 (Jonathan Torgovnik), 18 (Dan Lamont), 21 (Vincent), 23 (Jean-Paul
Pelissier/Reuters), 24, 26 (H. David Seawell), 31 (Carlos Lopez-Barillas), 35 (Steve Klaver/Star
Ledger), 37 (Macduff Everton), 41 (Bernd Thissen/dpa), 43 (Christinne Muschi/Reuters), 44 (Tony
Kurdzuk/Star Ledger). Corbis Sygma: 33 (Collart Herve). EASI-Images: 29 (Rob Bowden). Rex
Features: cover background (Yan Morvan), cover top inset, 9 (Duncan Ridgley), 13 (Ray Roberts),
15 (Luigi Narici), 38 (Garo/Phanie).

Printed in China

1 2 3 4 5 6 7 8 9 10 09 08 07 06

Contents

CHAPTER 1

Choking on Garbage

It is 2025 and the United States is facing a major crisis. The amount of garbage produced every year is increasing rapidly. Landfill sites are full, and incinerators are operating beyond their capacity. Garbage is piling up in the streets, and garbage collectors are threatening to go on strike. The government is preparing for outbreaks of disease caused by the litter lying around and by contaminated water. Rats skittering through heaps of garbage are now common in the cities.

At the end of the twentieth century, environmentalists urged governments to do something to reduce garbage and to consider the impact on people's health and the environment. The response was to double the number of incinerators and find new sites for landfills. More recently, officials relocated a village to create more space for garbage. The people who had to move are the first garbage refugees of our time! While scientists are looking into ways of sending garbage into space or burying it in the seabed, too many people keep throwing away valuable resources and filling their garbage cans every day.

Too Much Stuff, Too Much Waste

The disposal of garbage has become a serious issue in many countries around the world. How did we end up in this mess? All animals create garbage, but in nature, what is garbage for one species is food or a resource for another. Earthworms, for example, feed on dead plants; vultures eat animal carcasses; and dead animals decompose, helping to create rich, fertile soil. Our early nomadic ancestors produced very little garbage. Most of their garbage, such as food, wood, bones, and ash from fires, was biodegradable. Microorganisms such as fungi or bacteria broke down the garbage naturally, and it became part of the earth again. The change from nomadic hunter-gatherers to farmers meant that garbage was no longer left behind, and methods of garbage

TONS AND TONS OF GARBAGE
In 2000, humans produced 13.9 billion tons (12.6 billion tonnes) of garbage, more than 2.2 tons (2 tonnes) per person; by 2050, we will probably produce 29.4 billion tons (26.7 billion tonnes).

Source: *Tunza*, UNEP magazine for youth

disposal had to be created. Archaeologists have discovered the world's first municipal landfill in Athens, Greece, created in 2500 B.C.

The problem is that we are now producing more garbage than our natural environment can absorb, and an increasing amount of our garbage is nonbiodegradable. Since the beginning of the Industrial Revolution in the eighteenth century and the development of machines, we have learned to produce large quantities of artificial materials such as nylon and plastic. The development of new technologies has given us such products as microwave ovens, powerful cars, digital television sets, computers, and mobile phones. If we throw these products away, many of them will take thousands of years to break down—and some have parts that will probably never fully break down. The piles of garbage keep growing, and we add more to them every year.

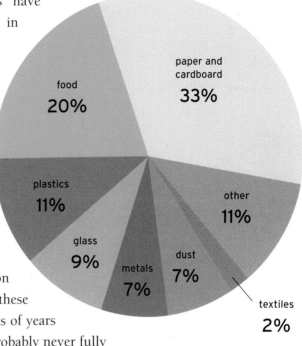

paper and cardboard 33%

food **20%**

plastics **11%**

glass **9%**

metals **7%**

dust **7%**

other **11%**

textiles **2%**

The graph shows what an average household garbage can in Great Britain contains. More than half the contents could be recycled or composted.

Source: Waste Watch

This beach in Majorca, Spain, is covered with garbage that has been washed up by the tide. Litter is a common sight everywhere around the planet. Materials such as plastic and metals that do not break down easily can be carried long distances by ocean currents and winds, ending up far away from where they were produced.

All Kinds of Garbage

Garbage can take many different forms. It can be solid and visible, such as the contents of your garbage can or the local city dump. It can be liquid, such as water contaminated by chemicals used in a paper factory. Waste can also be gas, such as the emissions from cars and power stations. Most governments classify garbage as *municipal* and *industrial*. Municipal solid waste is the garbage collected by local authorities from our homes, schools, offices, stores, restaurants, and hospitals. It makes up less than 10 percent of the waste produced in

Chemicals from industry and agriculture wash into ponds, rivers, and lakes, killing fish and other aquatic life. This lake in Kunming, China, has turned green as a result of such pollution.

industrial countries. Industrial waste, the main source of waste, comes from mining and quarrying, energy production, factories, construction, and agriculture. For every ton (tonne) of garbage we create when we throw an item away, 22 tons (20 tonnes) are created at the stage where raw materials are mined to produce it. Another 5.5 tons (5 tonnes) is created at the manufacturing stage. For example, just to produce a Playstation, a rare metal called tantalum that is used in circuit boards needs to be mined from the mountains of the Democratic Republic of Congo, leaving behind tons (tonnes) of mud sludge and large amounts of the chemicals used to separate the metal from its ore.

What Happens to Our Garbage?

What happens if you throw an empty can of soda into the garbage can? If you live in the United States, Canada, Great Britain, or Australia, a truck will probably pick it up and drive it miles away to a landfill site, where it will gradually sink into the ground. If you live in Japan or Denmark, it will probably burn up in an incinerator.

HOW LONG TO BREAK DOWN?

These are estimates of how long it will take for different items to decompose. The times vary depending on such conditions as the amount of sunlight or rainwater.

Material	Example of decomposition time
Cans	Eighty to one hundred years
Cardboard	Several months to five years
Cigarettes	Twelve to forty years
Disposable diapers	One hundred years to never
Fruits and vegetables	Six months to two years
Glass bottles and jars	Never
Paper	Five months to fifty years
Plastic bottles	Fifty to one hundred years to never
Motor oil	Ten to thirty years

Source: UK Composting Association and Waste Watch

A Trip to the Landfill

Dumping garbage in landfill sites has been the easiest and cheapest option for most industrialized countries. A landfill is a structure built into or on top of the ground where garbage trucks dump their loads of waste. The garbage is compacted and covered with a layer of soil to reduce odors and vermin. Landfills are not designed to break down garbage, merely to bury it. They are like giant storage containers that slow down the process of decay and protect the environment from contamination. Every day, the landfill gets more and more full as more garbage is brought in. Eventually, it fills up, is covered with soil, and becomes a permanent feature of the landscape. Closed landfills have been turned into parks, parking lots, golf courses, and even ski slopes. When a landfill is full, the garbage must go somewhere else.

TREATMENT OF MUNICIPAL SOLID WASTE (FIGURES 2000/2001)

Country	Total million tons (tonnes) per year	Landfill	Incineration	Recycling	Other (compost etc.)
United States	231 (208)	56%	15%	22%	7%
Japan	60 (55)	6%	73%	14%	7%
Germany	54 (49)	25%	22%	27%	26%
Great Britain	38 (35)	80%	7%	12%	1%
Switzerland	5.2 (4.7)	6%	47%	33%	14%
Denmark	3.8 (3.5)	10%	52%	22%	16%

Source: OECD, Environmental Data, 2004

Old Landfills for Sale

Until the 1970s, most landfills were crude garbage dumps used for the disposal of both municipal and industrial wastes. Very few people thought about health and environmental concerns. In 1978, events at Love Canal near Niagara Falls in the United States revealed that heavy metals, chemicals, and oil can seep out of old dumping sites many years after they have been covered. This seepage is known as leachate.

The increasing amount of garbage we throw away in industrialized countries means that landfill sites, such as this one in Britain, are quickly becoming full.

From 1920 to 1953, Love Canal was used as a dump for industrial waste. Then, the site closed, and the canal area was covered with dirt and presumed safe. It was sold to build new housing and promoted as a dream community. Gradually, toxic, or poisonous, chemicals and gases seeped out of the ground, contaminating land and water and causing severe health problems for the residents. Eventually the whole community had to relocate, and the area was cleaned up. Love Canal is just one of many serious cases of contamination that have brought public attention to the issue of waste.

The Problem with Landfills

Landfills take up space. They also cause pollution. The breakdown of organic waste inside a landfill produces gases such as methane and carbon dioxide that contribute to global warming. In many countries, new rules require the collection of methane gas from landfills. The gas from some landfills is collected, treated, and sold as a commercial fuel. Other landfills burn the gas to generate steam and electricity. The design of modern landfills prevents leachate from escaping into the groundwater. Nevertheless, environmentalists argue that landfills are time bombs; their contents slowly release into the air we breathe and the water we drink.

Up in Smoke

In many countries, especially in places such as Japan where space is limited, incinerators burn a lot of the garbage. Incineration is more expensive than using landfills, but it takes less space than landfills, and many people consider it a safer method. Various types of waste can be burned, such as tires, plastics, and chemical substances. Like landfills, however, incinerators can cause health and environmental problems. The burned materials do not simply disappear. Burning the waste pumps heat, toxic ash, and gases into the atmosphere. Modern incinerators can recover some of the heat generated in incinerators to produce hot water and electricity. Environmentalists argue, however, that incinerators are wasteful at generating energy, producing more carbon dioxide per unit of energy than an old-fashioned, coal-fired power station. When waste goes up in smoke, we are left with large quantities of toxic ash that still need to be

Toxic pollutants from the chemical industry are spreading to the most remote parts of the planet, such as the Arctic and deep oceans. On August 12, 1999, in the northern Arctic Sea, Greenpeace launched its Down to Zero Toxics campaign with the goal of eliminating toxic substances.

disposed of somewhere. Every 110 tons (100 tonnes) of burned garbage leaves behind one-third of its weight in ash.

Dumping in Rivers and Seas

Although it is against international law, people still dump toxic and industrial waste in rivers, lakes, and oceans in many parts of the world. Newspapers often report stories of factories dumping their waste into rivers or shipping it out of territorial waters to be dumped at sea. The dumping of everyday waste produced on board ships and military vessels is also a serious issue. Currents and tides may carry this pollution thousands of miles, and fish and other marine animals can ingest pollutants that then build up in their bodies. High levels of toxins have appeared in the fish and seals that are part of the diet of the Inuit, living in the Canadian Arctic. These toxins from industrial pollutants and pesticides have passed through the food chain but were originally discharged thousands of miles away.

Space Junk

We are not only polluting our planet, we are also producing garbage in space. With the development of satellites for telecommunications, military purposes, and astronomy, more and more debris from old rockets and satellites is orbiting Earth. When a satellite goes into space, the rockets that shoot it into orbit are discarded. A collision with even a small fragment of space garbage can damage a satellite, shuttle, or space station. In 1996, the French military satellite *Cerise* became the first casualty of space junk when it collided with the debris of a rocket.

WHAT WOULD YOU DO?

You Are in Charge

Following your government's proposal to build new incinerators, you are taking part in a regional meeting with other young people and representatives from government, industry, business, and environmental groups to discuss the problem of waste. Some initial ideas are:

- The government needs to force change and make manufacturers responsible for the waste they produce.
- Local authorities need to make recycling easier for households, stores, schools, offices, and hospitals.
- Individuals should be made to pay for the waste they produce.
- New technologies and methods of waste disposal should be explored, such as burying waste deep in the seabed.

Which options would you put forward to tackle the garbage crisis?

See the discussion on page 47 for suggestions.

CHAPTER 2

A Chemical Cocktail

It is 2025. A catastrophic accident occurred when some toxic waste in India exploded. It was the worst environmental disaster in history, with consequences no one can predict. Thousands of people have been killed or seriously injured, and the death toll is likely to rise dramatically over the next few years. The accident polluted many of the country's rivers, and drinking water is now running short. People have evacuated towns and villages and are living in temporary shelters.

For the past forty years, environmentalists around the world have urged their governments to make laws to restrict the use of toxic chemicals. Industrialized countries, however, have continued to produce more and more toxic waste. In spite of international agreements, many countries have continued to export their waste illegally to places that have no rules on toxic waste. The leaders of forty countries, including representatives from some of the main polluters, have gathered today in Washington, D.C., to draw up an action plan to stop the production of toxic waste and to ban international dumping.

Toxic Waste

Hundreds of millions of tons of toxic waste are produced and transported around the world every year, presenting a danger to people's health and to the environment. Waste is toxic or hazardous if it is flammable, corrosive, explosive, or contains poisonous substances. Most toxic waste comes from the production of chemicals and plastics, and about 90 percent is produced in industrialized countries. You are likely to find products with toxic components in your own home, such as batteries, computers, oil-based paint, cleaning products, pesticides, and weed killers. Problems start, however, when these products are broken apart or release their toxic ingredients into the environment. Such

MAKING A COMPUTER

The manufacture of one computer uses 66 gallons (240 kg) of fossil fuels, 49 pounds (22 kg) of chemicals and 413 gallons (1,500 kg) of water.

Source: UN University, Tokyo

waste needs special handling for treatment, storage, transportation, and safe disposal. In recent years, as controls on waste disposal have tightened in many countries, companies have begun to export their toxic waste to countries with better treatment facilities or less stringent regulations. In addition, products that are banned in many industrialized countries, such as asbestos, are still exported to developing countries where they can be sold.

E-waste

Since the 1980s, the high-tech boom has created a new type of toxic waste. Unwanted and unusable electronic and electrical equipment, such as computers, television sets, VCRs, DVD players, game consoles, stereo equipment, and mobile phones, appear in our dumpsters as often as new products to replace them appear on the store shelves. Electronic waste, or e-waste, contains toxic materials, such as plastics and heavy metals, that can release poisons into the environment. Computers and electronic games are made of more than one thousand different materials, and some of them contain toxic components such as lead, mercury, and cadmium.

The average computer has a lifespan of less than two years, and software companies constantly produce new programs that fuel the demand for more speed, memory, and power. Today, it is often cheaper and easier to buy a new machine than to upgrade an old one. In 2002, the number of personal computers in the world reached 1 billion, and sales continue to rise at a rate of about 130 million a year.

The WEEE (Waste from Electrical and Electronic Equipment) man stands in London. The statue is 23 feet (7 m) tall and shows how many electrical and electronic goods the average person in Britain throws away in a lifetime—more than 3.3 tons (3 tonnes).

WHAT'S IN A COMPUTER?

A computer is made of:

Material	Percentage
Ferrous Metals	32%
Plastic	23%
Nonferrous Metals (lead, cadmium, antimony, beryllium, chromium, and mercury)	18%
Glass	15%
Electronic Boards (gold, palladium, silver, tantalum, and platinum)	12%

Source: UNEP

Millions of cell phones with short lifespans are produced each year, adding to the pile of high-tech junk. The cadmium from one cell phone battery is enough to pollute about 158,000 gallons (600,000 liters) of water—about one-quarter of an Olympic swimming pool. When people replace these high-tech products, they simply dump most of them in landfill sites or burn them in incinerators.

Export of E-waste

In many industrialized countries, strict health and safety rules and high labor costs make the handling and recycling of toxic e-waste components extremely expensive. As a result, many of these countries export their e-waste to countries such as China, Pakistan, and India, whose laws are not as strict and whose labor forces are cheaper. The United States ships as much as 80 percent of its recycled e-waste to Asia. Computers, printers, television sets, and other e-waste sent for recycling are dismantled in enormous yards, where thousands of people try to make a living by breaking up the electronic equipment and recovering valuable materials such as copper, steel, plastic, and aluminum. Some of the plans that offer ways of reusing obsolete computers can be misleading. Probably, up to 75 percent of the computers and electronic goods shipped to Africa for reuse is actually junk that cannot be repaired or sold. Much of this equipment ends up in open dumps, or else it is burned, posing health threats to local populations.

An E-waste Village in China

Until recently, the Chinese village of Guiyu, in the southern province of Guangdong, based its economy on rice cultivation. Since 1995, however, Guiyu has become a booming

THROW-AWAY PHONES

About 105 million phones are replaced every year in Europe. If you placed them one in front of another, they would form a line 9,134 miles (14,700 km) long, enough to reach from Cairo to Cape Town and back again! Standing on top of each other, they would be 342 times higher than Mount Everest.

Source: www.weeeman.org

TYPE OF E-WASTE PRODUCED IN INDUSTRIALIZED COUNTRIES

Type of E-waste	Percentage
Refrigerators	20%
Information and Communication Equipment such as Cell Phones	15%
Electronic	15%
Monitors	10%
Televisions	10%
Other Electric Appliances	30%

Source: Basel Action Network, 2001

e-waste village. Although rice still grows in the fields, all other available space is used for recycling e-waste. Recycling involves taking electronic equipment apart and separating out useful materials. Workers open toxic products such as computers and printer cartridges without any goggles, gloves, or masks to protect them, because their employers do not worry about safety and protection of the environment. The average wage is about $1.50 per day. Computer parts are burned to recover precious metals such as copper and gold, constantly filling the air with black ash. As a result, many people have developed respiratory and skin problems. Tons of toxic residues are dumped in surrounding fields, ponds, and rivers. In 2000, water samples from a local river revealed lead levels twenty-four hundred times higher than the recommended guidelines for drinking water. The villagers now import their drinking water from a town 30 miles (48 km) away. Fishing ponds near the village are polluted. Guiyu is a shocking example of the impact of the e-waste trade.

Many children in the village of Guiyu, China, take electronic waste apart to help their families earn a living.

Responsible Recyclers

The leaders of government, environmental organizations, and industry are all trying to develop new measures to prevent the export of e-waste and to encourage recyclers to be more responsible. For example, in the United States, the Rethink Initiative helps sellers find takers for their unwanted technological gadgets through the auction Web site eBay. Rethink also offers solutions for the problems of how to recycle responsibly. The Silicon Valley Toxics Coalition has launched a campaign to make manufacturers take full responsibility for their products. New computers with lead-free circuit boards and plastic components made from vegetables are coming onto the market. In 2004, California added a fee to the price of all new computer monitors and television sets to cover the cost of recycling. In Europe, the first e-waste recycling system was introduced in Switzerland in 1991, beginning with the collection of refrigerators and gradually including all other electric and electronic appliances.

In 2006, the European Union (EU) adopted the Waste from Electrical and Electronic Equipment (WEEE) directive. This guide sets recycling goals for different appliances for EU countries and makes producers responsible for the recycling of their electrical waste. Another European directive bans new electrical and electronic equipment that contains certain toxic substances, such as lead. Many Asian countries, including Japan, South Korea, and Taiwan, have adopted similar laws that require that sellers and manufacturers pay for the cost of recycling.

Ship-Breaking

The ship-breaking industry is another major source of toxic waste. As industrialized countries have started to approve stricter environmental laws, ship-breaking activities have moved to countries such as India, Bangladesh, Pakistan, and China. About 50 percent of the ships in the world that are no longer used are recycled in Alang, a coastal town in India. The second-largest ship-breaking operation is in the port of Chittagong in Bangladesh. Large oil tankers, rusty car ferries, and chemical carriers are brought onto the beach during high tide and, as the tide goes down, hundreds of workers take the ships apart with blow torches and sledgehammers. They try to salvage what they can: steel, copper, useful machinery,

and furniture. Many of these vessels contain toxic materials, however, and the coastal waters around these ports are heavily polluted with asbestos, heavy metals, oil, and chemicals. Workers earn about $1.20 a day for this dangerous work, which exposes them to extreme heat, toxic and flammable gases, and dangerous chemicals. Usually they work without any protective clothing.

The Alang and Sosia ship-breaking yard in Gujurat, India, is the largest in the world, employing 35,000 migrant workers. The rate of accidents is very high due to gas leakage, explosions, and lack of protective clothing.

Nuclear Waste

Like all industries, producing energy creates waste. Radioactive waste from nuclear power stations is highly toxic and has been generated for decades. Although it makes up less than 0.1 percent of the world's waste, it is a major source of concern. Nuclear reactors split atoms of uranium to release energy. The spent radioactive fuel and the old reactors are extremely dangerous. Some high-level radioactive waste, however, will take more than twenty thousand years to decay. Since the invention of nuclear power in 1942, scientists have been looking for ways to get rid of such waste, which is currently being stockpiled in specially designed containers.

NUCLEAR FACTS

In 2004, radioactive waste was produced by 442 nuclear power plants, operating in thirty countries and supplying 16 percent of the world's electricity.

The vast majority of nuclear plants are in the United States, Canada, and Western Europe.

The seventy-five commercial nuclear sites in the United States will have 93,700 tons (85,000 tonnes) of spent fuel by the 2030s, well above their current storage capacities.

Only temporary storage methods exist for the disposal of radioactive waste, and none of the countries producing nuclear waste has so far managed to find a permanent solution. Long-term storage deep underground is one possibility, but the problem is that the earth moves, and no one can judge precisely where or when earthquakes will take place. The United States government has already approved a potential site for the disposal of nuclear waste at Yucca Mountain in the desert landscape of Nevada, about 93 miles (150 km) from Las Vegas. The proposed site will store all the high-level radioactive waste produced in the United States deep below

The United States government hopes to store high-level radioactive waste in this underground tunnel inside Yucca Mountain, Nevada. Many people are strongly opposed to the project.

Earth's surface in an underground tunnel. The plan is to transport waste by rail to Yucca Mountain by 2010. Like many nuclear facilities, the project is very controversial, and many people are strongly opposed to it, especially local residents.

A Poisonous Legacy

Serious accidents can happen with nuclear reactors that cause the release of high levels of radiation. In 1979, a reactor overheated at the Three Mile Island nuclear plant in Pennsylvania. Although there were no casualties, it stirred up public concern over the safety of nuclear energy. In 1986, a blast ripped through the nuclear power plant of Chernobyl, in the former Soviet Union, killing more than fifty-six people and affecting the long-term health of thousands more. The explosion at Chernobyl was the worst accident in the history of nuclear power. A cloud of radioactive waste drifted over northern Europe and beyond. Today, many farms across the north of Europe are still contaminated by the Chernobyl fallout. A fire at a Japanese fuel-reprocessing plant in 2000 and an undetected leak of radioactive materials at Sellafield power station in Britain in 2005 renewed concern over nuclear safety.

WHAT WOULD YOU DO?

You Are in Charge
You are delighted to get your new iPod player after months of saving money for the latest and most powerful model. The question is, what will you do with your old model, your old CD player, and your old sound system?

■ Give them to a thrift shop.
■ Throw them in the dumpster, because they do not work very well.
■ Leave them in your drawer or the attic in case you need them one day.
■ Put them in a special recycling bin for electronic goods.

Which option would you choose? How will it affect people and the environment?

CHAPTER 3

Living in a Material World

It is 2025. During the past twenty years, new laws have gradually been adopted in the United States and Europe to make producers pay for their garbage. Manufacturers and businesses now have to cover the cost of handling the waste that they create. Successful consumer campaigns have forced manufacturers to withdraw some products from the market because of their toxic content or excessive packaging. Governments have forced manufacturers to reduce the amount of packaging on other products and to make use of compostable materials. Environmentalists are delighted. The extra costs, however, mean that many businesses are in danger of closing down. Other businesses are threatening to move their operations to places where environmental laws are less stringent, to remain competitive. Many jobs have already been lost, and the price of electronic products is set to increase by 15 percent in the next two years.

A Disposable Planet?

As we aspire to improve our standards of living, we produce more garbage. The cell phone market is a good example of our throwaway society. In Britain, people replace their cell phones on the average of every eighteen months, even though a phone could last for up to eight years. About 15 million cell phones are replaced each year, and many of the unwanted phones are simply thrown away. Disposable goods have become part of our lives, from toothbrushes to cameras, pens, plastic cups, tissues, and batteries. In China, people throw away 90 billion disposable chopsticks every year, using more than 25 million trees and bamboo plants annually.

History of Packaging

More than half of what goes in our garbage cans is packaging. Today almost everything we buy and produce is heavily wrapped in layers of paper, cardboard, plastic, glass, steel, and aluminum. Fancy packaging started during the Industrial Revolution in Europe, when factories made mass production possible, and trade began to flourish between countries. New technologies and materials were developed to preserve and transport food and products safely and efficiently around the world. The invention of refrigerators and microwave ovens resulted in the development of heavily packaged fast food and convenience food, contributing to the mountain of garbage. Through the Internet, we can now order books, furniture, electronic games, and clothes from all around the world, safely delivered in packaging to our doorsteps within a few days. What is it all costing the planet?

PACKAGING MATERIAL IN MUNICIPAL SOLID WASTE IN THE UNITED STATES

Material	Percentage of Total Weight
Paper/cardboard	52%
Plastics	16%
Glass	14%
Metals	6%
Mixed Materials	12%

Source: USA Environmental Protection Agency, Facts and figures for 2003.

Bottling

Think about what you drink every day. How many plastic bottles, cans, and glass bottles do you use? Our early ancestors drank out of leather flasks or carved wooden vessels and used leaves for wrapping and storing their food. The invention of synthetic materials has enabled us to create different forms of packaging that are more hygienic and resistant to extreme temperatures. In 1944, a Swedish designer called Ruben Rausing created a new kind of milk container made of plastic-coated paperboard as an alternative to breakable glass. In 2003, Tetra Pak, Rausing's company produced 105 billion packages that are used around the globe to store and transport goods such as fruit juice and milk. Such packaging is essential for the modern food industry. In developing countries, where packaging is often minimal, 30 to 50 percent of the food produced rots before it even reaches consumers.

Food packaging contributes to the mountain of waste we produce every day. In 2001, in Britain alone, households produced the equivalent weight of 245 jumbo jets per week in packaging waste.

The problem is that plastic containers and cartons form a bigger and bigger part of our municipal waste. In Western Europe, 61 percent of the total plastic waste comes from packaging. Because of public pressure and financial benefits, major companies are starting to reduce the weight and volume of their packaging and use materials that can be recycled or composted.

A BRIEF HISTORY OF PACKAGING

Timeline	Invention
Pre-1800	Sacks, chests, and barrels are used for transporting and storing bulk goods
1800-50	Individual cartons and cardboard boxes are introduced
1840	Airtight metal cans are widely used
1852	First machine for making paper bags is invented in the United States
1880s	Mass production, folding cartons, and color printing allow companies to develop recognizable brands
1892	Metal tubes for toothpaste are introduced
1894	First Coca-Cola bottles are produced
1907	First commercial plastic is invented
1920s	Potato chips are sold in tins to keep them fresh Cellophane is used extensively for wrapping items such as candies
1923	Birdseye makes first frozen foods, sealed in cartons and wax paper wrappers
1933	Polythene is invented by ICI, a British chemical company
1940s	Aerosols becomes popular Plastic is introduced as a packaging material
1950s	Tetra Pak invents a germ-free milk carton Polythene bags are widely used
1970s	Many new plastics are developed for packaging, including the PET (plastic) bottle for carbonated drinks
1980s	Convenience-food packaging increases, including special designs for microwave ovens
1990s	New plastics can be put in a hot oven for cooking food New technologies in packaging help preserve food longer

Battle of the Bag

Most households have a cupboard full of old plastic bags. Although these bags make up a small proportion of our garbage, they have become a real problem for the environment. According to the nonprofit organization Clean Up Australia, Australians use more than 6 billion plastic bags per year. If they were tied together, these bags would form a chain long enough to go around the world thirty-seven times. Most of these bags end up in landfills, stuck on trees, or floating in the ocean, and they can take up to one thousand years to break down. Plastic bags pose a real danger for wildlife both in the marine environment and in the countryside. Tens of thousands of whales, birds, seals, and turtles are killed every year as they often mistake plastic bags for food such as jellyfish.

Different countries have adopted a range of measures to discourage the use of plastic bags. For example, in Ireland and areas of Australia and China, shoppers have to buy their plastic bags instead of being given them for free. In other countries, such as India and Bangladesh, plastic bags have been completely banned because they have blocked drains in cities and made floods worse. The ban has lead to a revival of the burlap bag industry. In South Africa, the government allows only the production of more durable plastic bags, hoping that the extra cost of these bags will push retailers and consumers to use fewer bags more often.

In southern France, sheep graze in a field covered with plastic bags blown by strong winds from a nearby garbage dump. Plastic bags, whether thrown away deliberately or blown from open garbage dumps, create many problems for wildlife and the environment. They end up blocking drains, trapping birds, and killing animals.

The Hidden Story of a Product

Every day people buy or use compact disks (CDs) to listen to music or play games on their computers. Have you ever thought about how CDs are made, what materials are used, or what happens to them when you do not want them any more? Looking at the life cycle of a product such as a CD helps to understand the connections between natural resources, energy, waste production, and wider environmental issues such as climate change. Garbage is created at each stage of production, starting with mining and processing raw materials all the way to the product's final use when you buy a CD. We need to find good solutions for disposing of garbage at every stage.

Making products such as CDs and DVDs consumes natural resources, produces garbage, and uses energy. Changes in the way we produce, use, and dispose of products could make huge reductions in garbage.

Production of a CD

1. Extraction of Raw Materials

Various materials go into making a CD, such as aluminum, plastic, glass, gold, silver, nickel, chemicals, and water. All must be mined, gathered, or made. Each material has its own life cycle, involving the use of natural resources and energy and the creation of waste.

2. Processing

Materials mined from the earth must be processed before manufacturers can use them. For example, bauxite is changed into a substance called alumina, which is then turned into aluminum. This process creates a highly toxic waste called *red mud*. To make plastics, crude oil from the ground is combined with natural gases and chemicals in a manufacturing plant. Making plastic generates toxic waste and emissions. Then, all the raw materials must be transported to the place where the CDs are manufactured.

3. Manufacturing

A machine creates the core of a CD disk—a piece of plastic, 0.4 of an inch (1 millimeter) thick. Melted plastic is poured into a mold, and the machine stamps it with tiny indentations containing digital information. These allow the CD player's laser to read the CD. The CD is then coated with layers of aluminum and plastic to protect against scratching and corrosion. Most CDs have a decorative label, and the printing process involves the use of different materials such as stencils and ink.

4. Packaging

CDs are packaged in clear or colored plastic cases or cardboard boxes and covered with plastic shrinkwrap. This packaging can be made from recycled or raw materials. When CD cases are broken or no longer used, they often end up buried in the ground or burned in incinerators, producing toxic emissions.

5. Transportation

Once the CDs are packaged, they are ready to be sent to distribution centers and retailers. They are transported by trucks, trains, or planes that use fossil fuels for energy and produce greenhouse gases.

6. Disposal or Recycling

Properly stored and handled, most CDs will last for decades or even centuries—until a new technology makes something better! Then they will probably end up in a cupboard, buried in the ground, or burned. The good news is that the use of iPods and Internet downloads is already reducing the waste created by the manufacturing of CDs.

CD FACTS

In the United States alone, more than 50 tons (45 tonnes) of CDs become obsolete or unwanted each month. More than 55 million boxes of software go to landfills and incinerators each year.

Several companies in Europe and in the United States now recycle old CDs and DVDs into high-quality plastic for reuse in products ranging from car parts to office equipment.

One recycling business in San Jose, California, processes 1 million CDs every month.

Source: Worldwatch Institute

Closing the Loop

To reduce waste, manufacturers need to *close the loop*, which means they need to reuse materials in the manufacturing process and convert unwanted waste into useful resources wherever possible. Closing the loop not only reduces waste but also helps conserve resources and save energy.

Beams and pipes made of recycled aluminum are ready for shipment in Virginia.

A good example of closing the loop is the town of Kalundborg in Denmark, which has developed a unique system of reusing waste. Factories, businesses, and the municipality have worked closely together since the 1970s to use each other's waste materials and surplus energy. For example, the oil refinery supplies its treated waste water to the coal power station for use in its cooling process. In return, the power station supplies the refinery with steam for use in its refining process. The waste gases from the refinery are used as fuel for the power station and for two nearby factories that produce plasterboard and chemical substances. Steam from the power station provides heat to a local pharmaceutical company, whose sludge waste is used to make fertilizer.

Clean Production

Since the 1990s, environmentalists, progressive businesspeople, and some government officials have promoted the concept of clean production. Clean production is not just about making things in factories in a cleaner way to reduce toxic waste. It is a way of looking at the impact of design and consumption on the environment. Cleaner products are being designed to last longer and to be reused, with minimal use of energy, water, and raw materials. For example, Hewlett Packard has developed a safe cleaning method for computer chips using carbon dioxide instead of toxic solvents. In 1999, IBM introduced the first computer that used 100 percent recycled resin instead of plastic. Companies are redesigning their packaging by using nontoxic and recyclable materials and by using fewer materials. In 2002, Nestlé UK changed the packaging of many of its products and saved 264 tons (240 tonnes) of metal and 230 tons (208 tonnes) of paper and board in one year.

WHAT WOULD YOU DO?

You Are in Charge

You work for a major cell phone company and have been asked to look at creative ways to reduce packaging and waste. The following ideas are being discussed:

- Invest money to research new forms of biodegradable packaging
- Provide incentives to increase the recycling of packaging materials
- Create cell phones that last longer and encourage consumers to keep them longer
- Make thinner and lighter packaging out of recycled materials

What would be your priority? Can you think of any other ways of reducing packaging?

CHAPTER 4

A Different View of Garbage

It is 2025. An old man is sitting with his grandchild on the veranda of his house in Nairobi, Kenya. "When I was young," he says, "I lived with my mother and seven brothers and sisters on the edge of the city. I stopped going to school when I was eleven years old to help my mother on the dump. We had to sift through garbage all day long, hoping to find something that could be reused or recycled. I used to cut myself all the time, and I had to carry a heavy bag on my back. Next to the garbage dump was a mountain of old tires that nobody seemed to want. It gave me an idea. Today, I employ one hundred people to make sandals, rubber boots, and bags from recycled tires. My company has formed cooperatives in five African countries, and we sell our products everywhere in the world via the Internet. I have seen similar businesses starting up in America and Europe where dumping old tires has become a real problem. I go to conferences all over Africa to tell my story and encourage other people to follow my example. One day, my child, this business will be yours. You will never have to pick through other people's garbage to earn a living as I once did."

Less Wealth, Less Waste

Industrialized countries, where only 16 percent of the population lives, produce more than half of the world's municipal waste. The average person living in the industrial world consumes nineteen times more aluminum, fourteen times more paper, thirteen times more iron and steel, and ten times more gasoline than someone who lives in one of the poorer countries. If the rest of the world consumed as much as people who live in the industrialized countries, we would need four extra Earths to provide the materials! Consumption is increasing rapidly in countries with fast economic growth, such as China and India, and so is garbage production. In poorer countries in Africa, Asia, and Latin America, where resources are limited, repairing, reusing, and recycling remains common practice.

- Municipal authorities collect only 25 to 55 percent of all garbage produced in large cities.

- More than 5 million people die each year from diseases related to poor garbage disposal systems.

- Approximately 3,858 tons (3,500 tonnes) of garbage are produced every day in Dhaka, the capital of Bangladesh. About 51 percent is collected and transported to open dumps; 26 percent ends up in backyards; 11 percent is left on roadsides and in open spaces; 9 percent is recycled by garbage pickers. Only 3 percent is recycled where it is created.

Sources: United Nations; Dhaka City Corporation

Items that go in the garbage in some countries are useful resources in Uganda. Kitchen utensils and lanterns are made out of recycled materials.

Garbage Factories

Amadou lives on the outskirts of Dakar in Senegal. Like millions of people in Africa, he lives in a slum on the edge of the city, between mountains of old tires and an old woman's store that sells plastic containers and scrap metal. Like many, he has left the countryside to find employment and a better life in the city. His home is made of the materials he could find and reuse, and he has no formal address. He has no basic services such as running water, toilets, or electricity. The city does not collect garbage in the city's outskirts, so mountains of waste build up. People in the community dispose of their waste in any way they can. They burn flammables and throw the rest into rivers, ditches, or streets.

In Amadou's world, garbage is a resource. Wood and metal scraps are useful materials for his home, and empty tin cans become water containers or toy drums for his children. All over the world, city dwellers make two to three times more garbage than rural people, although many cities in developing countries have poor facilities for disposing of waste. Most of the garbage ends up in the streets and in open spaces. Up to 95 percent of the garbage that is collected is thrown into open dumps. City garbage collectors do not, however, drive their trucks into Amadou's settlement.

GARBAGE PICKERS

Up to 2 percent of the developing world's urban population survives by scavenging. Each day in Kolkata, India, twenty thousand garbage pickers scour every square yard (meter) of the city's dumps, collecting garbage. High rates of infection and disease among garbage pickers in Mexico City give them a life expectancy of thirty-nine years compared with sixty-seven for the general population.

Source: *Tunza* UNEP magazine for youth

Living in Other People's Garbage

Bantar Gebang is one of the largest garbage dumps in Jakarta, the capital of Indonesia. The dump has been closed and reopened many times, as the city government has tried to cope with the disposal of the city's garbage. People who live near Bantar Gebang have long campaigned for its complete closure, but they are fiercely opposed by the garbage pickers, who make a living by sifting through the waste brought by garbage trucks from all over the city. The garbage pickers search for plastic, glass, metal, and cotton. They sort their pickings and sell them to dealers of various materials. The homes of the garbage pickers stand on the edge of the dump. They are made of scrap wood, corrugated iron, and any other materials the garbage pickers can find. A wooden shed with chicken wire for windows serves as a school. The children go to school in shifts. When they are not in school, they help their parents on the dump. They have frequent accidents and often develop diseases such as typhoid and tetanus.

A Global Phenomenon

Garbage pickers are a common sight in many developing countries, where large numbers of men, women, and children collect, sort, and sell garbage from households, streets, factories, dumps, and rivers to make a living. These people play a vital role in the recycling chain but are often either ignored or forgotten. Making a living from other people's garbage also occurs more and more in the large cities of North America and Europe. Rapid expansion of cities—along with a lack of housing and increase in population—has resulted in a growing number of people living on the street in extreme poverty. Many of them are children who have run away from home. Homeless people often use the garbage they find as shoes, clothing, and bedding. They also exchange cans and bottles for money and sometimes eat scraps of food from street dumpsters or fast-food outlets.

A man collects plastic items for recycling in an improvised shed on Guatemala City's main garbage dump.

Getting Organized

Cooperatives of garbage pickers are emerging across Latin America and Asia. Once organized, groups can strike bargains for better prices for the garbage they collect and make deals for good contracts with municipalities, governments, and businesses. In Colombia, a nonprofit organization called the Fundación Social helps garbage pickers form cooperatives and provides loans and advice to new organizations. One of these cooperatives is made up of one thousand garbage pickers. Sixty percent of its members are women. They earn one and one-half times the minimum wage and qualify for loans, accident insurance, and scholarships to continue their studies. In the city of Pune, India, a cooperative of five thousand garbage pickers has been appointed to organize daily door-to-door garbage collection from houses and offices. In Rio de Janeiro, Brazil, women have formed a cooperative to make use of their sewing and crocheting skills. They transform old fabrics into clothes and household products such as lamps, rugs, pillows, and sofa covers. Similar networks are developing in Argentina, Indonesia, Mexico, and the Philippines.

Cairo, Egypt, has a unique garbage collection system. Garbage collectors and recyclers known as *zabbaleen* collect up to 3,300 tons (3,000 tonnes) of household waste each day. The zabbaleen originally came from southern Egypt and migrated to the city to earn their living by turning municipal waste into resources. Without the help of government or outside agencies, they set up a door-to-door collection system, with each family working on its own daily route, to collect and separate household garbage. They resell recyclable materials at market rates, they give food scraps to pigs, and the rest of the garbage goes to a landfill. Most of the zabbaleen's income comes from the sale of recyclable materials, and they recycle 80 percent of the garbage they collect. The zabbaleen's way of life is now threatened by government plans to contract a foreign multinational company to collect and landfill all of Cairo's garbage.

WHAT WOULD YOU DO?

You Are in Charge
Think of the story you will tell your grandchildren in sixty years about the day when the waste crisis reached its peak, and the country came to a halt. The garbage collectors stopped collecting the garbage because protesters prevented them from getting to the incinerators and landfill sites. The government started to charge huge taxes to collect the garbage from your home. Your family and neighborhood had to find creative ways to reduce the amount of waste produced. What actions did you take on that day?

A Visionary Mayor in Brazil

In Brazil, the mayor of Curitiba has set up a unique system of garbage disposal with his citizens. Faced with full landfills and mountains of garbage, he decided to borrow money to build a recycling plant for the city. Curitiba's citizens separate their garbage into just two categories, organic and inorganic, and two different kinds of trucks pick up the garbage. A campaign in schools and neighborhoods has encouraged people to recycle and separate their garbage before collection. Poor families living in squatter settlements bring their garbage bags to neighborhood centers, where they exchange them for bus tickets, eggs, milk, vegetables, and fruit. Schools receive notebooks and toys in return for their metal, glass, and paper. The garbage goes to a plant, built out of recycled materials, that hires unemployed people to separate bottles, plastic, and cans. Two-thirds of the city's daily waste goes through the plant. Local industries buy recovered materials. The recycling programs cost no more than the old landfill, but the city is cleaner, the program creates jobs and supports farmers, and poorer people get help with food and transportation.

The inhabitants of the squatter settlements outside Curitiba, Brazil, receive food vouchers and bus tickets in return for their garbage.

CHAPTER 5

War on Garbage

It is 2025. The Smith family have been working for ten years to achieve zero waste. Zero waste is the name given to a radical approach to minimize and recycle waste at home, school, and work. It means using products longer, recycling materials, and composting organic waste. It also means reducing the pressure on the world's forests, soils, and mineral resources. The Smith family promised to incorporate the three R's into their daily routine—reduce, reuse, and recycle. This promise has changed their lives. They walk and ride bicycles, use public transportation or, if they really need to, their electric-powered car. They compost organic waste and recycle cardboard, paper, fabric, plastic, glass, and cans. They try to buy in bulk to reduce the amount of packaging. Most of their clothes are made from organic compostable cotton and recycled synthetic materials. They wear fashionable hemp and natural rubber shoes. The modern furniture in their house is nontoxic and made from recycled bottle tops and biocomposition, a material stronger than oak. Part of their pledge is to persuade at least ten of their friends and neighbors to commit to achieving zero waste.

Reducing Garbage

The best solution to the garbage crisis is to reduce the amount of garbage we create. Our daily choices determine the amount of garbage we produce. Although our garbage cans represent only a small part of the total waste generated, it is an important part. Changes in the way we buy, use, and dispose of products could make huge reductions in garbage. The first question to ask ourselves is whether we really need to buy a new product or throw away an old one. We can give old computers, sound systems, books, and clothes to friends, family, or thrift shops or sell them on the Internet. When we buy things, we can reduce garbage by avoiding overly packaged goods, and we can take our own shopping bags to the store to reduce the use of disposable plastic bags. We can also make sure that we buy nontoxic, durable, and recyclable products or products made of recycled materials. Buying printer cartridges that can be refilled, for example, reduces toxic waste.

Sustainable Consumption

As consumers, we have considerable power, and we can make a real difference. By changing our shopping habits, we can put pressure on businesses and industries to rethink the way they produce and package their products. Sustainable consumption is about using goods and services that meet our basic needs and create a better quality of life for all while minimizing waste, pollution, and the use of natural resources. It is also about sharing resources between rich and poor and acting with concern for future generations.

A boy recycles a bottle at his school. We produce and use twenty times more plastic today than we did fifty years ago. Recycling plastic is becoming more popular, transforming old bottles into new everyday items such as fleeces, CD cases, or filling for sleeping bags.

FANTASTIC PLASTIC?

Plastic is one of the most commonly used materials today because it is light and strong and does not break easily. Did you know, however, that:

- It takes one full cup of crude oil to make the plastic for each disposable diaper?
- Toothbrushes represent more than 99 million pounds (45 million kg) of plastic waste each year?
- Recycling a single plastic bottle can conserve enough energy to light a 60-watt light bulb for up to six hours?
- Recycling plastic saves between 65 and 80 percent of the energy required to make new plastic? It also saves two-thirds of the sulphur dioxide emissions.
- It takes about twenty-five recycled plastic bottles to make one fleece jacket?

Source: www.zerowaste.co.nz

A Different Destination

If we cannot reduce or reuse, then recycling is a good option. Go back to that can of soda you threw in the garbage can. What would happen if you had put it in the recycling bin instead? A recycling truck would have picked it up and dropped it at a center that sorts cans, glass, paper, and plastic. Along with other cans, it would have been squashed into big bales and taken by another truck to the aluminum can factory miles away. At the factory, the bales would have been shredded into small pieces, cleaned, melted down, and rolled like pastry into thin sheets. Then it would be ready to be made into new cans.

Did you forget to put your can in the recycling bin? That is what happens to 80 million food and drinks cans every day in Britain. Like everything else that is bundled into garbage bags, they just end up in landfills or incinerators. Making one new aluminum can takes the same amount of energy as recycling twenty cans. Britain alone would have 12 million fewer garbage cans to empty each year if all aluminum drink cans were recycled.

Recycling

In industrialized countries such as the United States and Britain, almost half the contents of our garbage cans could be recycled. Recycling means changing waste into usable resources. It can involve turning old material into a new version of the same thing or into something completely different. For example, glass bottles can be recycled into new bottles, or plastic bottles can be used to make fleeces.

Recycling only works, however, if there is a demand for the recycled products. Many people believe that things made from recycled materials are of lower quality than products made from new materials. As a result, in many countries, usable materials pile up in recycling plants. Another problem is that plastics are difficult to recycle and should be separated before being tossed in a recycling bin. For example, milk and dishwashing soap bottles are made from a different kind of plastic than margarine tubs and

---

RECYCLING

Did you know that:

- The energy saved by recycling one glass bottle will power a computer for twenty-five minutes or a television set for twenty minutes or a washing machine for ten minutes?
- Recycling seven steel cans saves enough energy to power a light bulb for twenty-six hours?
- Producing an aluminum can from recycled material can save enough energy to run a television for three hours?

grocery bags. If they are not separated carefully, the plastic cannot be recycled.

Composting

Composting is a simple way to recycle. Composting is the natural breakdown of organic matter by microorganisms into a rich material that makes a great natural fertilizer. At least 20 to 50 percent of the waste sent to landfills is made up of tree leaves, grass clippings, and kitchen waste. Bagging these materials for garbage collection costs a lot of money and has an impact on the environment. Many countries collect organic material separately and take it to municipal composting sites. Even with a small amount of space outdoors, however, you can reduce the amount of waste you put in your garbage can by separating your organic waste and using it to make your own compost.

An organic farmer in Wisconsin holds a handful of red wigglers. This type of earthworm is often used in composting to help turn organic waste into rich, fertile soil.

Recycling is Cool

Everyone should buy recycled products. Innovative companies are constantly coming up with exciting designs for products made from recycled materials. In 1993, Patagonia, a well-known American outdoor clothing company, was the first to use fleece made from recycled plastic in its product line. Since that time, Patagonia has saved about 86 million soda bottles from the garbage heap. In 2003,

A giant stack of textiles awaits recycling. Reuse and recycling of textiles is now a major industry, and products made from recycled materials are appearing in the fashion industry.

Sotheby's, an auction house in London, promoted waste as a material for creating exciting designs through a contemporary art and design exhibition. The exhibition included clothes using gold-sprayed coffee filter bags, mirrors made of decorative scraps of materials, and a selection of quirky lamps made of old machine parts. Stylish bags from recycled materials such as plastic, car upholstery, juice box labels, and skateboard decks can be bought in fashionable stores. The company Relan, for example, turns old billboards into handbags. Pencil cases and computer mousepads are made from the rubber from discarded tires. In Canada, you can buy copies of some of the Harry Potter books that are printed on 100 percent recycled paper.

At the Fashion Show

Reusing and recycling textiles is an old idea, but it is now a big industry. The clothes we wear and the textiles used to make them can have a huge impact on the environment. For example, the pesticides farmers use to grow cotton, the chemicals manufacturers use to dye textiles, and the old clothes that we throw away all contribute to waste. Most of these clothes could be recycled or reused.

The good news is that clothes made from recycled materials are now appearing in fashion shows. In Denmark, Earth A'Wear was the first shop to stock only *green* clothes; these clothes are made from environmentally friendly or recycled materials. Some skirts are made from pineapple fibers and belts from bicycle tires. In 1995, the Italian designer Armani started to recycle old jeans into new ones. Armani has since created a line of clothing made from hemp, a fast-growing plant that is environmentally friendly because it needs no pesticides or herbicides, uses little water, and does not deplete the nutrients in the soil. The German adventure sports manufacturer Salewa produces clothes made from corn. The corn is fermented to produce a fibrous substance. The clothes made from this material are lightweight and breathable, and when their owners are finished with them, they can go into the compost heap.

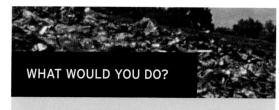

WHAT WOULD YOU DO?

You Are in Charge
Think about a day in your life and all the things you buy, consume, and throw away. Try to identify three actions that would help to reduce garbage at home or at school. How would you persuade friends and family to take action?

CHAPTER 6

Time to Change

It is 2025. World leaders are gathering in Beijing for a third Earth Summit. The garbage crisis has become a global problem, and the agenda will focus on action toward sustainable consumption. Sixty percent of the countries that submitted a report for the first Earth Summit in 1992 said that solid waste disposal was one of their biggest environmental concerns. More than thirty years later, most governments have failed to take enough action to address the waste crisis. They have simply dug more holes in the ground to bury garbage and built more incinerators to burn it.

Since the last summit, groups of young people have come together all around the world to initiate real action in their homes, schools, and communities. In their view, not enough has been done in the last twenty years, and they are putting pressure on governments to give them a genuine voice at the Beijing Summit. They are asking governments to adopt a zero-waste approach. They are trying to persuade big companies to introduce the concept of clean production. Young people want to have a genuine voice at the summit to present their views because they will be the decision makers of tomorrow.

Zoom around the World

In the twenty-first century, environmental groups and bodies such as the European Union are putting pressure on governments to take real action. In many countries, new programs encourage people to reduce waste and to recycle. Here are a few examples of what happens to garbage in different places around the world:

Switzerland

In Switzerland, throwing garbage away costs money. The Swiss have to pay for the number of garbage bags they fill. About 47 percent of the municipal waste is recycled or composted. Retailers and producers recover recyclable materials. Electronic goods, such as computers, TVs, and refrigerators carry a recycling tax, and toxic waste is sent to special sites.

Denmark

In Denmark, garbage is a resource. Garbage is taxed if it goes to landfills and incinerators, but it is exempt from tax when it is recycled. Packaging, plastic bags, and batteries are taxed to reduce e-waste. More than one-third of all household garbage is recycled. The total amount of garbage is not big enough for Denmark to have its own recycling plants, however, so plastic, e-waste, batteries, and metal are sent abroad for recycling. The government encourages industry to reduce waste and subsidizes cleaner technologies.

Germany

In Germany, the polluters have to pay. Different types of materials are collected for recycling. Legally, toxic waste, such as batteries or chemicals, has to go to special recycling centers. Manufacturers have to take back their packaging. Consumers pay a deposit on packaging that can be recycled, such as cans and plastic bottles.

A German worker sorts electronic waste along a conveyor at a processing center. In Germany, electronics manufacturers bear the expense of recycling. Electronic equipment, from cell phones to deep freezers, is collected and sorted at processing centers like this one.

Ireland

Ireland introduced a tax on plastic shopping bags in 2002. The tax has persuaded shoppers to reuse their bags. Irish shoppers now use 90 percent fewer plastic bags.

United States

In the United States, methods of garbage disposal and recycling rates vary from state to state. More than six thousand cities have adopted pay-as-you-throw programs, in which residents pay for the amount of garbage they produce. Recycling rates have almost doubled during the past fifteen years. In San Diego County, California, all materials that can be recycled are banned from landfills.

Senegal

In Senegal, recycling is not left to industries. It is part of daily life. Everything is reused or recycled, from plastic bags to school notebooks, tin cans, plastic bottles, and organic waste. Tin cans become drink cups, and old newspapers wrap food. Artisans use metal waste to produce anything from chairs to children's toys.

China

China offers tax breaks to companies that recycle waste or use recycled products. China has recently put a tax on disposable chopsticks, sold in billions every year, to reduce waste and the use of timber. Taxes have been raised on luxury items such as yachts, large cars, and wooden floor panels.

Latin America

Clean power plants operate in Brazil, Argentina, Chile, and Venezuela turning biomass (plant and organic matter) into electricity for more than five million customers.

One World

The garbage crisis is a global problem that needs a global response. Countries have come together to agree on clear targets to tackle the problems associated with waste. For example, in 1989, the Basel Convention was created by the world community to control the movement of hazardous waste from one country to another. The agreement specifically aims to prevent rich, industrialized countries from dumping their electronic and toxic waste on poorer countries. The convention, signed by more than 150 nations, came into force in 1992 with the goal of reducing the creation of toxic waste and disposing of it as close to its source as possible. The United States, however, has yet to ratify the agreement, even though it creates one-third of global toxic waste.

TACKLING WASTE

Statements from international agreements relating to waste:

"Environmentally sound management of hazardous wastes or other wastes means taking all practicable steps to ensure that [such] . . . wastes are managed in a manner which will protect human health and the environment against the adverse effects which may result from such wastes."
Basel Convention, 1989

"Overall objective . . . To prevent or minimize the generation of waste. This should be part of an overall cleaner production approach; by 2010, all countries should have national plans for waste management."

In 1997, the Kyoto Protocol set a goal for reducing emissions of carbon dioxide and other greenhouse gases by 5 percent by 2012. Although some industrialized countries, such as the United States and Australia, have not yet agreed to the protocol, it still marks an important international commitment to reducing emissions that contribute to global warming. Even though these goals are not always met, they are a huge step forward because they indicate a commitment from nations around the world to reduce emissions and highlight areas where progress needs to be made.

A cyclist rides past a wall mosaic installed by the environmental pressure group Friends of the Earth outside the United Nations Climate Change Conference in Montreal in November 2005. The words Make Kyoto Live Today! *remind politicians of the targets set in Kyoto to reduce greenhouse gases.*

An Agenda for the Twenty-First Century

Agenda 21, an action plan for the twenty-first century, was adopted by 179 nations at the Earth Summit in 1992. It devotes three specific chapters to the problem of waste. Agenda 21 says that we need to reduce waste, recycle, and tax packaging materials. Industry needs to adopt cleaner production methods, and new technologies should be made available to developing countries. Agenda 21 also talks about the importance of informing people about the risks of the chemicals they are exposed to and the need to clean up contaminated areas and help their inhabitants. It supports the idea of making polluters pay and promotes a ban on the export of toxic waste to countries not equipped to deal with it. Agenda 21 promotes adopting sustainable patterns of production and consumption. It urges a halt to the excessive use of natural resources, such as wood.

Zero Waste

Zero Waste is a new approach to waste based on the idea that we can eliminate garbage altogether. As the world's population continues to rise, the system of using up resources to make packaging and products that will later be burned or buried is not sustainable. Zero Waste is a different way of looking at things. It goes beyond recycling and entails redesigning products and changing the way waste is handled so that products last longer and materials are recycled. Waste is seen as a resource and means jobs for people, money for businesses and industries, and material for new products.

In some industrialized countries, such as Canada and Australia, leading corporations, municipalities, and governments have united

Tom Szaky is the cofounder of TerraCycle, a company that produces organic plant food. Organic waste is fed to millions of worms. The natural fertilizer they produce is then liquefied and bottled in used soda bottles. This product is entirely made from and packaged in waste.

in adopting strategies toward a Zero Waste society. The goal is to reduce the amount of toxic waste they produce and to conserve and recover all resources. Zero Waste means no waste goes to landfills and incinerators. It means that producers are responsible for the products and packaging they produce, and that consumers must reuse or buy recycled products. It means that governments must provide financial incentives for consumers and producers to reduce waste.

Zero Waste in Action

An increasing number of cities and states have adopted the goal of Zero Waste, including Canberra in Australia, Toronto in Canada, and the state of California in the United States. In 2002, New Zealand became the first country in the world to adopt this strategy. What we need, however, is to have industries, businesses, communities, and countries all over the world working together to increase recycling, reduce waste, reduce consumption, and ensure that products everywhere are made to be reused, repaired, recycled, or composted.

PLEASE REUSE THIS BOOK!

It takes approximately seventeen trees to make 1.1 tons (1 tonne) of paper, not to mention large amounts of water, chemicals such as chlorine and sulphur, and energy. Please make sure that when you have finished with this book, you pass it on to a friend.

WHAT WOULD YOU DO?

You Are in Charge
You are a member of a youth delegation representing your country at the Summit on Sustainable Waste. What actions will you take?

- Identify the main problems in your own environment with your friends, family, and teachers.
- Suggest an action plan on how you can encourage waste reduction.
- Challenge your leaders to bring the waste issue to the center of local and national decision making.

Glossary

Agenda 21 An international agreement to reduce the impact of human action on the world's environment

asbestos An inflammable mineral made of long fibers that is resistant to chemicals; it is used as a heat-resistant material; asbestos can damage people's health if the fibers get stuck in their lungs

bauxite The mineral that is used to make aluminum

biodegradable waste Waste that breaks down or rots naturally when attacked by bacteria; examples include food and garden waste

biomass Plant material or agricultural waste used as a fuel or energy source

cadmium A metallic element found mainly in zinc, copper, and lead ores

climate change The process of long-term changes to the world's climate, increasingly as a result of human activities polluting the atmosphere

compost A mixture of organic household garbage (for example, vegetable peelings and brown cardboard) and plants that have decomposed over time

consumption The use of resources, products, and services by consumers

contaminate To pollute or expose to radioactivity

corrosive Describes a substance that can eat away or consume metals by chemical action

emissions Gases released into the atmosphere

ferrous metal Metal that contains iron

fossil fuels fuel formed in the earth from plant or animal remains

global warming A gradual warming of the surface and atmosphere of Earth; evidence includes the melting of glaciers, the rise of sea levels, and an increase in the temperature of the atmosphere

greenhouse gases The gases that trap the Sun's heat and warm Earth such as carbon dioxide and methane; human activity has increased the level of these these greenhouse gases in the atmosphere accounting for much global warming

hazardous Describes something that is dangerous to humans, other living things, and the environment

heavy metals Metallic elements that can be harmful to living things and that tend to build up in the food chain; heavy metals include chromium, mercury, cadmium, arsenic, and lead

incineration The process of burning combustible waste, producing heat, gases, and ash; the heat can be used to generate electricity; incineration, however, also releases toxic gases.

landfill A site where waste materials are deposited into or on the ground

leachate Rainwater that seeps through a landfill and becomes contaminated; if not contained and managed properly, leachate can pollute groundwater, rivers, and coastal areas

methane A highly flammable gas released by landfill sites; methane contributes to global warming

microorganism An organism of microscopic size such as a bacterium

municipal solid waste The solid waste produced by homes, schools, offices, and stores

natural resources Substances of use to humans that are derived from the earth (for example, coal, wood, metal ores) or from living things

nonprofit organization An organization that is independent of government and whose goal is to provide a service, not to make a profit

nutrient Any of the minerals that are absorbed by plants or animals as food

organic waste Waste derived from plants and animals

pesticide A chemical used to kill insects and other pests

pollutant Something that contaminates air, soil, or water

radiation Energy that is transmitted in the form of rays, waves, or particles

radioactive Describes elements, such as uranium or plutonium, that give out radiation as they change into other elements.

raw materials The basic resources used to make materials and products; for example, bauxite is extracted from the earth to make aluminum

recycling Using materials that have been used before to make new things; materials that can be recycled include glass, paper, cardboard, steel, aluminum, and plastic

residue Matter remaining after something has been removed; for example, residues from incineration include toxic ashes

sustainable consumption Using goods and services that meet our basic needs and bring a better quality of life for all, while minimizing the use of natural resources, waste, and pollution; it also refers to sharing resources between rich and poor and acting with concern for future generations

toxic waste Waste that is poisonous to humans or other living things

Zero Waste A goal that, if met, would result in very little waste being created; instead, people would find ways to reduce the amount of materials used in the first place and to reuse or recycle unwanted materials

Further Information

Books

Bowden, Rob. *Waste, Recycling and Reuse.* 21st Century Debates (series). Hodder Wayland, 2003.

Gifford, Clive. *Waste.* Planet under Pressure (series). Raintree, 2005.

Morgan, Sally. *Waste, Recycling and Reuse.* Sustainable Futures (series). Evans Brothers, 2005.

Parker, Steve. *Waste and Recycling.* Green Files (series). Heinemann Library, 2003.

Web Sites

Environmental Kids Club
epa.gov/kids
A site for children produced by the Environmental Protection Agency, providing facts and action you can take.

Treehugger
www.treehugger.com
A web magazine that gives information on recycled products and discusses the impact of waste on the environment.

Waste Online
www.wasteonline.org.uk
A great source of information on every aspect of waste.

The WEEE Man
www.weeeman.org/
An initiative to raise awareness of the amount of electrical and electronic equipment the average person in Britain produces. The site allows you to measure your own impact.

YouthXchange
www.youthxchange.net
A web site full of information from all around the world about reducing waste and sustainable consumption.

Publisher's note to educators and parents: Our editors have carefully reviewed these Web sites to ensure that they are suitable for children. Many Web sites change frequently, however, and we cannot guarantee that a site's future contents will continue to meet our high standards of quality and educational value. Be advised that children should be closely supervised whenever they access the Internet.

What Would You Do?

Page 11:
Solutions to the problem of waste are not simple. When we bury or burn our garbage, we lose valuable resources and energy. Recycling can be costly and impractical. A combination of actions from consumers, businesses, manufacturers, and governments is needed. Many people believe that governments need to take direct actions that will force changes. They argue that by taxing wasteful and pollution producing activities, governments are able to influence businesses, industries, and individuals to change their attitudes toward waste.

Page 19:
When recycling electronic waste, you need to make sure that the waste is not sent abroad and that you deal only with responsible recyclers. To find out about programs in your local area, you can look at electronics-recycling directories on the Internet.

Page 27:
When considering the packaging of cell phones, these questions might be helpful. Is the item overpackaged? Is the package recyclable or made of recyclable material? Is it biodegradable? Can the package be recovered from consumers? Do cell phones need to be changed every year?

Page 32:
To help you with this subject, you could investigate what ends up in a typical household garbage can over a week. (Please make sure that you wear protective gloves when examining the contents of your garbage can!) What is the garbage that could have been recycled? How can you encourage everybody in your neighborhood to reduce, reuse, and recycle their garbage? For example, you could set up a task force in your local area with your neighbors and representatives from the government and local businesses. What actions could you take to encourage the government to tackle the crisis? You could suggest ideas for making recycling easier or making manufacturers responsible for the waste they produce. How can you target the industry and the business sector? For example, you could write letters to ask companies to stop sending junk mail that you do not want or to reduce the amount of food packaging that ends up in your garbage can.

Page 39:
Here are a few tips to reduce waste. Buy only the amount you need. Give preference to objects that can be recycled, repaired, or are reusable. Avoid disposable products such as plastic cups, cameras, and batteries that contribute to landfill problems. Avoid items that are overpackaged. Take your own bags to do your shopping to avoid using plastic bags. Recycle materials such as cans, plastic, cardboard, paper, and glass. Encourage family and friends to reduce, reuse, and recycle.

Page 45:
It will take more than recycling a few cans to sort out the problem of waste. You can participate in decisions that affect you. Make your voice heard. Find out what are the main issues related to waste where you live. Identify practical actions that you can take. For example, you could write to companies to tell them that you will not buy their products unless they reduce their packaging or use recyclable materials.

Index